Andra Simons is a Bermudian  in London. He studied theatre collection of poetry, *The Josh* published in 2009. He has performed at numerous festivals and events.

Turtlemen is typeset in Lato, a font described by its designer, Łukasz Dziedzic, as 'male and female, serious but friendly, with the feeling of the summer'.

Copy Press

Turtlemen

Andra Simons

The Copy Press Limited
51 South Street
Ventnor
Isle of Wight
PO38 1NG

copypress.co.uk

Commune no.14
Editorial: Cecile Malaspina,
Yve Lomax, Vit Hopley
Reader: Vanessa Jackson
Copy-editor: Sara Peacock
Design: Opal Morgen/John Peacock
Repro: Jono Lomax

Front cover © Michael Parsons

Printed on Munken Print White
no.18 80gsm. Munken Print White
standard products are FSCTM
and PEFC certified.

Printed and bound in England.

First edition © Copy Press Ltd/
Andra Simons, 2021

Andra Simons asserts the moral right
to be identified as the author of
this work.

A catalogue record for this book is
available from the British Library

ISBN-13   978-1-909570-07-8

All rights reserved. No part of this
publication may be reproduced, stored
in a retrieval system, or transmitted in
any form or by any means, electronic,
mechanical, photocopying, recording
or otherwise, without the prior
permission of the publishers.

This book is sold subject to the
condition that it shall not, by way of
trade or otherwise, be lent, re-sold,
hired out or otherwise circulated
without the publisher's prior consent
in any form of binding or cover other
than that in which it is published and
without a similar condition including
this condition being imposed on the
subsequent purchaser.

For Coralita

Contents

Preface

Who are your people? As asked of you by the old gossip-keepers when you venture out beyond your local tribe roads. They ascertained if you were worthy of association by the begets you had learned ever since you were old enough to utter syllables. After a round of ice-cold ginger beer, the elders would send you back home having recalled everything about those who had walked along your line before you, whose ancient tears you weep and whose rusty tone of laughter knocks the bells in your throat.

Our lineage is all we have, our lineage and our ghosts. We are a displaced people planted on far-away continents and small islands, yet our ancestorial stories persist in fragments, embedded in the tales told by those very gossip-keepers: the tales of Turtlemen. They are reimagined myth born in the absence of myth, in the absence of memory. They are resuscitation of myth.

Am I of the Turtlemen? I was born and reared on the islands of Bermuda, the cultural landscape from which I have drawn inspiration. I created Turtlemen (a tribe located on the western end of the island) within a dimension, existing beside and often merging with Bermuda's people, sharing their history, from 1700s brutalities to the turbulent winter nights of 1977 and to our present. Both dimensions have deep and shallow waters, and both serve as a ledge for the characters as well as me to leap off into the wider world.

Turtlemen is an essay on attrition and longing, a journal and eulogy. It is a saga of those that remain and build and of those who sail afar and search. Like Turtlemen, we must exist ourselves into existence.

Turtlemen

Turtlemen

HURRICANE: *Emily*

There are dogs in the wind. I am waiting for them
to die, circling around outside.

I hope they'll find holes deep enough in the earth
to feed and bark again.

There are dogs in the wind, I am waiting for them
to die, I'm waiting for them to howl

and bite back.

Prologue

GOSSIP-KEEPERS: Turtlemen learn how to whistle before they learn to swim, an ancient technique passed through the undertow. Our story tells us of those very long days. God had grown quite impatient,

he had become hungry for his beloved tribe of masons, those who had been trained to build empires yet neglected obscure green waters – trembling women and men weary of diving and retrieving

fragments of the new sun (the stuff of imperial mortar) from the bottom of the gluttonous ocean. Thus, God began to carve the sum of every empty attempt onto the backs of each fatigued diver

layer upon layer upon layer upon layer upon layer upon layer upon layer upon layer upon layer upon layer upon layer upon logic upon layer upon livery upon loss upon law upon

lament upon language upon lust upon lips upon layer upon layer upon layer upon layer upon liberty upon layer upon layer upon layer upon love upon layer upon layer upon layer

upon longing upon layer upon layer upon lift upon layer upon layer upon layer upon until each figure carried behind them their own uniquely shaped fleshy soft shelter.

Before every futile mission, each would hold onto the shoulder of the person on their right, turn and kiss each companion's forehead to their left and grasp that luminous line from the lip to the

gut. Together they resembled a wilted bay-flora garland at the water's edge waiting for the final wave. S>p>l>a>s>h

the rebellion crushed God against the reef, and they
whistled to drown out the splitting of the universe in two.

ME: My father too whistled. I studied the quiver in his
intensity and the rapture in each undulating hypnotic note.
I could only tightly press my lips and blow bubbles from
behind my small, sharp teeth. These are the neglected details
in child rearing: I never learned to rebel, trumpet a rally cry.
This space we swim through must never recover God.

Cherry Bush

When they come for us in their big-boy boats
I close my eyes under the shade of the cherry bush

We gonna run to the fort and flood our moats
I close my eyes under the shade of the cherry bush

Betty hide the 'quats and thread the ropes
I close my eyes under the shade of the cherry bush

And if they come aground with their purple throats
I close my eyes under the shade of the cherry bush

They'll slip on the slope and slit their coats
I close my eyes under the shade of the cherry bush

So, they better not come in their big-boy boats
I close my eyes under the shade of the cherry bush

Note: traditional Turtlemen's nursery rhyme

Dream of My Birth

Crackle. Crickle. Crackle. The soot settled just above the harbour at dawn the day my father gave birth to me. The rioters had torn down the walls of the justice hall. Looted and torched the warehouses of canned meat, lard, and black tyres. Hung bodies from Her Majesty's hotel balconies. They paraded on the asphalt and lit the centre yellow line with a flame. Who would dare to cross this disputed border? I was coming. I was coming. I was coming.

Crickle. Crackle. Crickle. A small-scale revolution scorching the walls of my grandmother's bedroom while my father already past his best-by date bit down on the white leather-bound New Testament according to King James, holding low the volume of God. My grandmother dressed in paisley gabardine and a scalded knife, cut my father's red bloom and reached into it. He's coming. He's coming. He's coming.

Her tar black hands pulled out the lump of molten rock, cooled it and dipped it in a bed pan of sea water; she then rubbed it with clouded shark oil before placing it on her tit until I suckled me out. It was then that the revolutionaries with petrol-covered hands holding on to pitchforks and machetes gathered ten metres reach from my slit father, lured by the aroma of sweet new rot. They all gathered and looked down at the wrinkled babe.

My small hands hit at my purple torso where there was an empty hole the size of a mother's fist. I had no liver, no bile; no place for blood to die nor a vessel for the breakdown of complexities.

Grandmother told one of the rioters to fetch her sewing basket from the linen closet. He returned. She threaded a camel-eyed needle with purple thread so that it matched my skin and cross-stitched upward turning a circle into a line.

She then told another boy to look under the kitchen sick and find the large empty mayonnaise jar, the one she had once used to store pickled beets; she warned him that he must bring it hot washed clean. He returned with the jar clean and dry. Grandmother took the jar from the boy's trembling hands and placed my baby arms around it, kissed my temple then whispered, 'Hold tight, this is yours to dispose of all your dark matter, hold on tight, hold on tight'.

Cadets

Family lore tells us he fought a Portuguese man-
o'-war and won. Tied. He grew to brawl. Tied.
Regardless from whose armada they belonged.
Tied to me. He remained tangled. Red flags on
stern as he tried to unknot himself.

Burn. Burn. Splash. Splash. War. War. Weapon.
Cannon. One. Needs only one. Turn. Break him.
Turn. Splash. Turn on me. Suck. Splash. Suck.
Splash. Suck. Suck. Cock. Splash. We tangle. Fold.
Spit. Spit. Push. Fit. Push. Hard. Push. He is hard.
Push rush rush this blood. Push huge teenage
cock into

I close my eyes under the shade of the cherry bush.

Boy cunt. Boom. Boy cunt. Boom. Right hand
wipe ass. Hands flush first blood. Kick. Kick at
the Boom. Break me. Clash make me. We tangle.
Man-o'-war. We tangle. We tangle. We tangle.
Wounded island boys search for any hole that
may hold fresh water.

I proposed a treaty and watched him drink.
Watched him break it. Red ink on my hands.
I reckon I should have learned to whistle...
blow. Blow. Blow those black sails in.

A Funny Boy stares into a 13" B/W TV

In sub-tropical winter 1977, I forgot I was a
boy. Tonkya and Johnny and the Archibald child
smelling of lemongrass and dried fennel, tossing
tennis balls against the wall ten times ten. I
stitched plump clouds by hand with acrylic thread
into Argyll shorts that would slip from my waist
after a midday downpour. One boy my Casuarina
pine pod, another my round conch Venus, and
the Archibald boy, a critter in my belly. Under the
Hibiscus bush I built my nest and searched for
snails, ant trails, and Princess Leia's mother's name
coded in cinema laser frequencies, marked on
ever-moving clouds.

December curfew. Radio from across the bay.
Gunshot-startled urban dwellers and country
kin gather in our small city to watch a brilliant
midnight supernova and calypso sounds of sirens.
Tourists exploded from flaming hotel halls. I
however painted a green gown on Lena Horne
as she strutted the black and white stage in a far
far away country. I twirled into a girl as my father
searched from beside the window. The revolution
would step onto the gallows at dawn. He knew
my secret; one day as a woman I'd bring the
coloureds in from the rain.

Prometheus Baygrape

Fire breathers, so the myth goes, with doe eyes
and men's ashen skin are born on isles too small
to spot on the colour-coded map of a breathless
empire; born in villages of strange stones buoyant
on a turbulent and limbless ocean.

They lick at their wings preparing to leap into the
brittle and knotted grey-haired sky, these odd
men who flare to mark the passing of sunsets
along the rows of banana groves.

This is the stuff we recognize in the opening chord
of our tiny songs.

***

Some men fear boys and the brave way their
cocks jump at the start. Big boys with their flat
chests, eel-black at the twist of an arm, a frolic of
thighs and shoulders, tongues wagging. Mmmm,
bravado of hatching manhood.

I knew Prometheus Baygrape walked these
touchstone beaches, near the guys who play ball
with the violent surf. But he dared to stand where
the ocean's white teeth rip at the shore, the scent
of their blood carried to high ground.

When he set himself alight, such a crackling
brilliance, that aching muffled bang, some thought
him a dragon, lighting other hearts aflame.

I feared most for him. Accident and Emergency
Units could only identify him by the pattern of his
teeth – each crooked crown – each glow for help.

***

I'm scarred by the one named Baygrape. He left
keloid crescent moons on my forearms when he
reached for me. I shhh his temper, trusting I'm too
old to remember the spark.

Prometheus: combustible brazen monk blazing
against this war and these poverties.

I fear most for men born of that strange glow,
their carbon claws clutching at setting embers.

Unca

On days that seemed as imperfect as they were
sunny, we knew him by the sound of his limp. He
was Momma's favourite brother, born with a bird
on his thumb. We could hear his intoxicated jazz
shuffle coming up the hill, a tall looming sun dial,
ticking on fate's window. He was bleached oats
soaked in whiskey for colour, his hair unwoven
threads of a kin's tapestry, always beating on our
panes tentative like a stranger. Strange, Momma
never seemed home for his visits. I swithered as
I opened the door; he would come in and sit.
And I, too afraid of this apparition of manhood
to speak, chose to stare hoping that somehow
I could infuse in him a spirit like the way he ate
onions as apples, like the way his fingers coiled
around half-empty bottles.

He marinated slowly with his head lowered, sitting
silent dripping, melting, decaying. It's funny how
kitchens become parlours for the dying, when life
is all we have left to devour.

Interlude

GOSSIP-KEEPERS: Turtlemen learned to grow large sweet onions. Learned to grow white lilies and how to build swift lean boats. Turtlemen learned to sturdy ships to spear whales. They learned

the movement of the tides and the mood of shoals. Turtlemen learned to bait, catch and boil. They learned to save the eyes for last. Turtlemen learned to milk their goats. They learned

to sleep next to the window and wait for the floral scent of forgiveness on the breeze. They learned their darker-skinned kin were not as revered as their paler-skinned conquerors. Turtlemen learned

to create coloured tiers of their own and build them into their constitution. Turtlemen watched as others were lured from the edge of the Sargasso to work their fields. Turtlemen learned

to pin the lips of their unmarried sisters. Turtlemen pulled socks up to their knees. Turtlemen are caul-bearers who learned to speak to their dead. They learned

to keep the rats away so they can bury their boys beneath the banana groves. Turtlemen learned to pray to the new god of the Adventists, who promised their boys will rise again. They prayed to the God of the Methodist and the Episcopal.

Turtlemen learned the delicate skill of praying to any god who will pay their rent. They learned to catch rain on rooftops and read hues of clouds to know when to pull the washing in from the line.

Turtlemen have learned there's no point in learning how to drown, it's quicker to die of thirst. Turtlemen learned to deny. Turtlemen don't talk about the scars on their back.

<Turtlemen don't talk about the scars on their back
<Turtlemen don't talk about the scars on their back
<Turtlemen don't talk about the scars on their back
<Turtlemen don't talk about the scars on their back
<Turtlemen don't talk about the scars
<Turtlemen don't talk.

Mangrove Folk

Mangrove Folk

HURRICANE: *Katrina*

She was black, with teeth. She knew how to use both.

Depending on the task she would choose the sharpest.

Harpoon

SCENE: 1730. The sound of a horse-drawn cart can be heard along with the voices of a jeering crowd. An elderly woman is walking toward a pyre. Her hands are held together and tied.

SARY: No need to hurry/ it won't happen till I get there/ I can see how you pile those cedar arms high/ light your torches in anticipation/ I see those eyes/ all hundred of 'em/ I see every single eye/ waiting/ waiting/ waiting for me to burn/ ol' black pig to roast/ I see your blue eyes turned grey/ those bays turned grey in the brewing storm/ I see those/ green eyes turned orange/ palms at dusk/ and those brown eyes/ black slaves broken at night/ worn at night/ those eyes ablaze/ all killin' time/ my blood ain't nothin' new/ ain't no different than swine/ or any other horse/ worked till it ain't nothin' but to put down/ ain't no different than any other chicken/ throat twisted and cut/ its body chasin' dreams of flight but always fallin' short/ ain't no difference/

I'm just another harpooned whale caught out there past the banks pulled into shore/ circled/ sealed in/ gasping outta water/ drying out/ outta water/ surrounded by all your tight/ taut/ faces bleached like sack cloth hardened like mud pies/ rippin' it open/ rippin' big black Sary open/ pulling me/ open/ fresh caught whale flesh/ unspoiled cold meat/ white bastards can smell unseasoned catch/ like salt fish sailing in from the Turks/ oh, don't you remember/ when you owned this body/ do you remember/ thought you could bottle me and sell me slowly piece by piece/ those years and years and years ago/ you can't see me now/ marchin' to hallelujah/

when I found out what you been doin' to my baby's baby/ Beck/ Beck/ it seems you philistines hadn't enough of me/

so you smell me out in my gran'baby/ you reach inside her and pulled out her soul/ she said she ain't got one no more/ you got hers and you wearin' it on your fingers/ pointing at her/ remindin' her/ she's yours/ her soul's at the tip of your finger and you pointin'

the lord tol' me to run to the devil/ this time my baby Beck/ she/ harpooned brought into shore/ I needed the devil/ not even the lord got power like Satan/ call me lover of Lucifer/ bride of Beelzebub/ throw me all your names/ they only strengthen my place/ you all/ worse than that Satan/ he don't like you neither/ says you are all devils of a different kind/ he never once asked to broaden the gap 'tween my dark ashy legs/ dip his sickle into my womb/ harvest his tribe/ NO/ he only asked me to bring him some of my cedarberry wine/ drink that makes prophets of the worst of us/ he only want some of that/ the way big black Sary makes it/ an' we talked/ long past midnight/ so long even the moon closed her eyes under the night shade of the cherry bush/ so far inside ourselves/ where the fresh waters run still/ where crystal fingers hold caves wide open so that voices roam unshackled by their bodies/ where my pulse ain't nothin' but a drum/ dum/ dumm/ dummm/ dummm/ remindin' me that death is always certain/ always lurking/ always/ waiting to make a friend/ the devil/ showed me the face of heaven and heaven she look just like me/ like me/ you hear/ like the night on a Sunday mornin' wakin' up knowin' she's got only one holy day off of her feet/ she look like a hundred mees/ like a thousand mees/ too many mees to count/ like the leaves of a match-me-can/ too many leaves/ an' I rounded all the mees I see/ all the men mees/ all the women mees/ even the children mees/ all those I could find with my face/ with my voice/ with my pains/ with my harpoon/ protrudin' out my ribs like our last oar to row us home/ those who I couldn't find/ who hid in the fennel bushes/ afraid of their mastas/ I sang that song out loud and let it whistle in the trees/ there was a rhythm in my whistles/ loud rhythms/ whistlin' drums/ even those weakened negroes couldn't ignore my rhythms/ run to the sea/ run to the sea/ and I went down to Hog Bay where I know there are gardens of death/ I picked me some herbs that pull sleep/ scored the dosage/ I found an ancient oleander/ leathered and thick/ sliced her breast/ poured one stone of her milk/ I gathered for three nights/ slept at the mouth of the Atlantic and roared back at her at daybreak/ I filled my skirts/ my shoes/ my satchels/ my scarves with the delicacies of death

[Sary is tied to the pyre. The crowd stands around: some jeer loudly; others stand afar in stillness]

I was delivered during a tempest in godforsaken hours/ beating outside my door/ screaming/ Witch/ Coon Conjurer/ pulled by the hair/ once again circled/ sealed in/ gasping' outta water/ drying' out/ outta water/ I had failed/ the ravagers of girlhood had not perished/ my drums had not unified/ I should have terrified them all/ but/ who betrayed these chains/ these chains who no more wish to be bond to us as we to them/ who betrayed these irons – free earth melted down and forged into links and cuffs/ which hell-licked nigger betrayed the irons/ I know that I am nothin' but withered ageing time/ I know that you must've feared for slave-kind and our rebel songs/ turned into children's play tunes/ without sting or reason/ I know/ I know why it's me you shut your eyes at in the crowing hour/ but why betray these irons

[The sound of crackling fire]

you all betta hurry there/ I think the sun wants to bake
me before you can/ she's a long-memoried queen/ she's
gonna make sure you don't forget the day Sary burned/
heat/ bitter lemon chorus/ aye/ may your sweat-stained
garments never dry/ you/ with skins of pigs/ may you
darken like field hands/ and the dead suckle your offspring
like mammies/ and as for my people/ they will find my name
on their tongues/ every day her majesty parches their skins
and lips/ leads them to thirst for something more/ and the
generations of my Judas/ who will soon kiss me with his
syphilitic flames/ may they never lose the weight of these
irons around their ankles/ wrist/ throats/ pullin' 'em down/
Beck/ Beck/ Beck/ They're gonna burn me now/ I'm gonna
burn for you/ I spared my soul/ here/ on my finger/ do
you see it/ staring/ pointing at you/ you are mine/ farthest
where the fresh waters run still/ where the caves hold
boundless voices/ take this harpoon out of my side and
row through this shit/ out from where it is thickest/ out to
where the stench turns to healing salt/ run to the sea/ see/
gran'baby/ rejoice/ run to the sea.

[She burns]

41

We are the Subtle Grip

We are the subtle grip
around the neck of these birds.
Their songs aren't silenced
just un-heard.

Note: traditional Turtlemen proverb

The Killing Floor

THE RUNT: We ate our mother. We were young and red then. We may not have known the season, but it was the same light every evening, when the blood drains from the dusk leaving the grey matter hanging above. Mother, her hair pulled back into a peppercorn sack, her day clothes unfastened, un-sized and clinging onto the dust from the yard. Exhausted, she hobbled in from the hours of peeling the husk from our onion home. She would pull out the potatoes from the dark cupboards below the sink and haul herself onto the polished teak chair that shared her weight intimately.

We never found time to wait. She would give us a pointless signal; a lift of her right arm, her left hand propping the least tender breast. She'd remove any drape from her neck, unsheathe her coconut-oiled thigh, one per night and we would leap. We learned to feed before we learned to breathe; each spotted sibling gnawing at her, piglets warring for too few teats, too little time. Sometimes she would flavour her meat with rose water, or garlic chives, sometimes paprika or frangipani. And as we would rip, chew and swallow, we'd grow fat and unable to walk on our own. Mother would grow a little more yella and limp, ageing as the speckled eve.

Her eyes would close like a carefully placed knife, her breath humming a cautionary tale. Sometimes I could hear her tear open, a little high apologetic note only sung by mothers and the slaughtered; and I could hear that my brothers could not.

Return to Sender

A canvas pouch of postcards: the Golden Gate
Bridge, the Empire State Building at night, the
Statue of Liberty, a lake near Reno Nevada and
a road cutting through a desert toward a flat
horizon which could be nowhere else but a
moving America. We pull them from under our
mattress every Saturday morning before we set
about our weekend chores. We lay them side by
side on the blue patterned carpet, creating a map
of unknowing.

On an out-of-date atlas our fingers trace
aeroplane departures, bus routes, taxicab
deviations, calculating journeys with very
little – weekend after weekend. We believe
we can predict her return. So, we wait for
confirmation from her America, with a picture
of her smiling beside some polished monument
too big for the photo. A smile that says: 'I wish
you were here with me', 'Missing you' and
'Sorry that I left, but Momma will be back
before the lilies bloom. I love you more than
you'll ever understand.'

We wish for that single card to be popped
through the door, perhaps bought for 10 cents
from a vendor along an avenue in Manhattan, or a
busy boutique near Haight-Ashbury. Or perhaps

she's waiting to design her own postcard with
XO around the border. Waiting for someone to
snap her. Waiting and waiting beside that carved
stone figure too threatening to be consumed in
a single shot.

Waiting with a smile that lingers on the face long
after that moment has passed. She's waiting with
her hands clasped behind her back displaying the
crisp dress she'd purchased to let us know that
she's fine, all fine. She's waiting to give the signal
for us to dash from the corners in our Sunday best
so that we can join her in the centre, waiting for
someone, anyone, to come along and capture all
three of us within the edges.

stretchMARKbirth

SCENE: A male figure. He stands in silence. He stares through a window. A woman can be seen sleeping on a bed. He climbs through the window, quietly, gracefully. Inside he stands looking at the woman sleeping. She is still. The man takes off his shoes and socks and is regimental in the way he places them under the window. He takes off his shirt revealing a scar that looks like an unlaced shoe that runs the length of his torso. He folds his shirt and lays it on the edge of the bed. He continues standing over the bed; a breath is left between him and it. The woman opens her eyes.

WOMAN: Snapper. That you?

MAN: [Silence]

WOMAN: Snapper? Oh God. Jesus. Christ. Help. Me. Help. What do you want? Please don't hurt me. Please.

MAN: [Silence]

WOMAN: Who are you? What do you want from me?

MAN: There once was an old Potter who, after one long day at the market bartering his wares, yet selling none, came upon a preacher man on a stoop just outside the market grounds. He was so caught with the power of this preacher and how he so loved his god, that the Potter was moved to create a vessel. He ran home to begin...

WOMAN: Who are you?

MAN: The Potter caressed and bent over the clay until the pot matured into form. He fired it and went looking for the learned preacher. When he found him, he said, 'look, I have created your god' and the preacher said 'take a lock of my hair, put it in your pot and cover it for three nights'.

WOMAN: The Lord never said that.

MAN: I never said the Lord said anything.

WOMAN: Who are you? What do you want from me?

MAN: Who is Snapper?

WOMAN: Never you mind who he is. Get out. Get the hell out. Get. Out.

MAN: Do you know you could see your reflection in the moon? **[Pause]** I'm not leaving till I get what I came here for.

WOMAN: What are you looking for?

MAN: [Silence]

WOMAN: What is it you want with me? I'm an old woman. Maybe you have the wrong house.

MAN: No. I don't.

WOMAN: If you're gonna do it. Please do it quickly.

MAN: [Silence]

WOMAN: Take me. But why would you? Look at my legs. I've walked a thousand of these hills with these legs. I've walked from the 50s into the new century with these legs and they're still not sore. Look at these arms. You want these arms? Take them...

MAN: [Silence]

WOMAN: Look at this neck, these breasts, I've never nursed a baby with these breasts. Do you want to be the first? Do you wanna suckle this tit? Look at these, bags of longing. Do you want to enter this? This... **[She begins to weep]** and this face, look at this face. This wrinkled...

MAN: And graceful, haunted face. Who's Snapper?

WOMAN: Don't you ever say his name – come take what you came here for. Do it now and then leave. Please leave.

MAN: I knew a woman once so frightened of her own reflection she wouldn't even swim on the north shore.

WOMAN: Why?

MAN: 'cause the water was so still she could see herself. For years she never cried because she was afraid of her gaze staring at her from the back of her hand when wet from wiping tears away. But she would look at the moon. For only those few nights every month, she'd see herself smiling back; silent, triumphant, honest.

WOMAN: What's that?

MAN: What do you mean?

WOMAN: The scar. What happened to you?

MAN: It's a birthmark.

WOMAN: That's not a birthmark.

MAN: How would you know?

WOMAN: Because I just would.

MAN: How would you know how birth marks you? [Pause] They removed my heart.

WOMAN: You're demented.

MAN: When I was born, I was too frail. I believe it was stolen.

WOMAN: And I suppose that's the reason you're here; you believe I stole your heart. Packed it up somewhere in my closet to rot away or dry out. Hung it upside down like dead roses. Over my door.

MAN: I know a man who for forty years, every Tuesday at 4:11am sharp, would climb through his neighbour's window. She was a beautiful woman who he believed had never truly seen herself.

WOMAN: Who are you talking about?

MAN: And there in her not-yet matrimonial bed they would hold each other, kiss, fondle those places that chime. He would leave his family to lose his body in her well. And she would say, 'look at yourself'.

WOMAN: Where are you going with this?

MAN: One Tuesday. I found her waiting. But she knew deep down he wasn't coming any more. Her water was gone.

WOMAN: Be. Quiet.

MAN: Now she wishes she had told him all the things she knew.

WOMAN: I want you to go. NOW. Or I'll scream.

MAN: Scream.

WOMAN: I will.

MAN: No one will hear you.

WOMAN: My neighbours are like morning glory, growing all over my walls and over my back.

MAN: Scream.

WOMAN: Don't dare me.

MAN: [He screams]

[Silence]

MAN: I want to be born with a new heart.

WOMAN: You're a... Freak. Somebody's going to come any moment.

MAN: Look at me.

WOMAN: I'm telling you to stay away from me. Don't. Don't touch me.

MAN: Look at me.

WOMAN: Don't hurt me.

MAN: Please. Look at me.

WOMAN: No. Don't...

MAN: Look. Look. Look.

WOMAN: ...Hurt. The moon.

[Pause]

MAN: I've come a long way; I want to come back in. Think of me like rum on a chilly day. Perhaps a bit of added sweetened ginger. Imagine it moving up inside you instead. Warm. Making you feel bold again.

WOMAN: Look how beautiful you are. I always knew you'd be this... divine.

MAN: [He stares intensely into the Woman's eyes] They took my heart, and the water went cold in the middle of August.

WOMAN: I knew you would return. Make him come back to me, please. For years I slept with my window so wide open, it had become a door. He would climb through. Spread my curtains wide and stare at me with those eyes. Those eyes. He was a fisherman. Spent days out at sea.

Alone. The silence of it all. How could he bear it? The ocean reflecting the whole sky under him. How silent and heavy he had become holding the universe at the end of his line. Those eyes. The eyes of a man who had watched his island disappear beyond the line a thousand times. When he climbed through those green curtains, I was his land, sand for his feet. But I never told him. He never knew just how soft and unsteady this ground was.

MAN: Here.

WOMAN: [Touching the scar] They cut so deep.

MAN: There's an ancient echo. If you listen close enough.

WOMAN: [She listens to his chest] I hear someone whistling that old-timey lullaby.

MAN: yet, Mother, my chest is empty.

WOMAN: So is mine.

MAN: Take me in. Let me crawl back inside. Let me grow teeth and hair and fingers and a heart again.

WOMAN: No.

MAN: Bones, dreams, a tongue

WOMAN: No

MAN: You left the window open.

WOMAN: You want to rip me open and climb inside. What

do I have to lose? You tore me apart coming out. I want you to give him back to me. Promise me that. Give me something to hold. Give me peace.

[She lays back and spreads her legs open as if she's about to give birth. The man circles her bed and then climbs between her legs. She breathes heavily. He moves into a foetus position]

WOMAN: It was easy. Not telling him. Keeping that secret to myself... Always on a Tuesday, he would come... I carried small. Hardly showed. He would tease me and say I was growing plump because of all that fish he was feeding me. Truth is I couldn't hold that fish down. The more he brought over the more I would become ill. But I forced myself to swallow it. The little secrets we keep down yet are forced to bring back up.

He never knew. Then I heard the baby's cry in the other room grow weaker and weaker. Its heart just wasn't strong enough they said. They tried everything. They even opened my baby... I have stretch marks, still, little street streams, or kite tails or cursive letters along my belly. Still, he never noticed it. Some secrets you learn to keep down. **[She whistles]** There was a woman once, she made a vessel out of clay, fired it and went searching for the preacher. She couldn't find him anywhere. So, she filled her vessel with tiny shiny objects, crystals in the gravel, the ocean during full moon – shhh, and those parts of her body which reflected light.

Seer

Momma claimed she had 'The Gift' and read
dreams like the ingredients of hand-me-down
recipes, heard ancestors' voices mixed within
the grey cricket and frog songs that peeped
when the world round and tight moved into
twilight. While fish-head chowder simmered on
our stove in a dented cauldron she sometimes
would stumble into fortune and drop her kitchen
instruments, like her parsley-flaked blade,
foretelling: 'A man's coming.'

We would giggle, her three sons and her,
knowing this is where Momma faltered. Never
did a man walk up our dirt road, pound out our
names on the front room door, or bring news of
death and grieving. She would pick the utensil up
and bless the earth onto which it fell. Years later,
contemplating many knives and the earth on to
which they fell I realize Momma had the gift
after all.

The men. They did comeandcomeandcome. They
came from behind shadows of the un-plastered
walls of construction sites. The mendidcome. Out
of bathrooms at the end of darkened corridors
where three-year-old lips taste salt and yeast
and urine. The mendidcome. Men who were
straitjackets. Men who violently imploded. Men
who cut.

Oh Momma the men have returned. They're pounding out my name leaving runaway trails on our dirt roads leaving news of deathanddeathanddeath.

A Blue Note for Daddy

My Daddy told me seven years ago, out of his
tipsy blurred soul, and pronounced with the
precision of negotiating narrow omnibus routes

'I was born a bastard and so forth are my children.'

I neglected to un-knot the lacings that tied me to
his boots at 1am in the morning, my un-etched
palms as bowls holding his drool. I wanted him to
drink-me-drunk, stumble through me.

Come sunrise, I yearned for my Dad who once
perfected backyard cricket, who often let me ride
behind his bus driver's seat until his shift closed;
I craved the father who stood wide shouldered,
wise over the toilet and demonstrated aim and
shake. It was his zealous rage fuelled by Gosling
Rum that sent her screams – womanish and
terrific with my tiny feet blistered by gravel at
runaway speeds.

'Bastards are hard to come by these days.'

Like him before, I am one: A broken, limp, soft-
shouldered figure – stripped and fat as my façade.

Counting Stones

My grandmother had almost drowned when she was a girl. In shallow water. When every other island girl was taught to swim, she taught herself to swallow brine, clap at the water, to never go down.

Those soft hands, the colour of cream-tea, collect stones where the sand meets the hard grass. Each is inspected under her thumb. She only needs one. Two. Three. Each one goes into her pocket. We are at the longest bay in the west, facing north. High tide has come in and we have drawn back.

My grandmother sits on the sand nearest the mangroves, where the water is shin deep. She unfastens her brown leather sandals and places them at attention beside her. Her faded lemon dress with the floral-patterned pockets seems strangely out of place here. Her eyes are fixed on me. I find a white clearing amongst the seaweed bed. I'd swim over those dark shapes beneath, afraid to put my feet down upon the slippery softness. I jump up and down, water at my waist, slapping an aquatic heartbeat with flat palms. When my grandmother is at the beach silence isn't an option. Her eyes remain fixed.

Through the years I had heard of fishing boats
named after great-grandmothers drifting back
home without fishermen. We knew they did not
go down easy. Or young folk daring on rock edges
as hurricanes closed in and nowhere to be found
when the storm closed out. Or those bartered for
and stored below ship decks one by four by black
millions along a well-mined passage towards so
called 'New Worlds'. Collateral to be dropped.
Heartbeat overboard. Silence at last an option.
Or an empty makeshift raft from a blockaded
island towards a rhinestone democracy. Or tens
of thousands called towards the Mediterranean
from the deserts and the jungles and the holy
lands. Dozens upon scores who sail inflated
vessels painted the same colour as passports,
flag stars and stretched tarpaulin. Washing up as
stones onto shore. Waiting to be gathered up by
grandmothers, where the sand has etched a hard
border between itself and the free grass.

This whale is a 27-metre-long, 90-ton, 104-year-
old. Charcoal black. Snow-grey broad markings
decorate her jaw, fins with tiny floral-like spirals
around her tail. She passes by the coast to sing
every year during whale-watching season. She
is a breaching whale with a mouthful of krill and
seawater; leaping onto the sheets of sky until her

tail dances tippy toe on the north horizon
before clapping hard onto the ocean's back;
then she goes swiftly deep, belly full of breath,
seeking out waterlogged ghosts who have
forsworn the surface. My grandmother is grace.
She is stealthy, gliding under pressure between
the layers of the dark Atlantic, until each open
mouth is accounted for.

New Year's Day

My father's mother delayed for me. She laid
patient, unblinking. My father's mother always
had a way about her that could tolerate a bad
taste in the mouth, an itch between the thigh,
or a grown cousin's spite smeared on the kitchen
floor. The mother of my father knew I'd be late
and out of breath at the church door because I'm
always behind the clock. She rarely went through
church doors but thought this day appropriate.

Sons of this son are disappointments, they can't
count money, they can't make babies, and they
can't keep time. Sons of this son can't fly. The
bells of St James toll out over the west and those
in black ascend; they've been gathering and
praying at the foot of the churchyard, sniffing
for rumours amongst the foreign baggage I've
brought with me. They want news as to why the
postponement.

My father knocks on the pew as to know we can
begin. His mother can't defer any longer. The
people want to sing hymns and holler 'Amen' at
the pastor. They want myth in her eulogy. They
want to beat my father's mother back to the fell
hands of God. My father's mother was hoping
I'll arrive before the bearers marched, before her
name is mis-spoken on the hour.

Pond
Peoples

Pond Peoples

HURRICANE: *Fabian*

A hurricane is a gentle thing when in the
centre of your lover's eye nothing stirs.

Parting the Atlantic

We, the Exodus Tribe, make preparations in the wee hours. There's a hush that holds our hands in muted motions. Our suitcases wait like hungry children at the door. We will leave this place at the same time the ocean gives up its body toward the moon and the shutters are opened on the eastward window – out of which god envies our escape. We've left his unmade bed to sprint over vine grass cooled by weeping lilies. Our lips stained by patience, which we could not let bitter our tongue.

Whores we will be, no longer. If only we could move under the sun. If only our nakedness could move through the street. Dreaming townsmen are dying tonight, suffocating within a pink painted fantasy, unaware the true dreamers are fleeing by boat.

We scuttle out of home, laden with everything we need:

✓   cedar-blood for our future doorpost
✓   frog songs
✓   warm sand under foot
✓   hymns (we haven't sung yet)
✓   my lover's open kiss

and prayers to a battled land, a stilling wait for
a dark long-tailed angel who in the mists of an
ageing foreign town will come to spook us again.

Canadian Rendezvous

My first love was a loon, who thought he was
a man, who thought he was a water buffalo.
In fact, he had only dated other water buffalo,
who pretended to be men, who I thought were
obvious loons. Even though I had told him many
times I was a descendant of the ancient tribe of
Turtlemen he often confused me for a tortoise. I
hadn't the tenderness to tell him the difference.

His thoughts were two-minute songs by blond
water nymphs bouncing on television; I yearned
for a singular thought of his own. On Saturday
afternoons he would splash-dive into a murky
lagoon beside the motorway under a cloudless
sky. Holding his breath, ballooned, he'd twist
and turn underwater, smear his feathers in grit
churned up from a soft bottom. Returning, his
head would rear out with a popping bellow,
arching proudly his imaginary golden bowed horns
that he believed were conduits of the divine.

After his ritual, he would come onto the bankside
beside me, dripping beneath a temperate sun
and smile as if he had found a chorus whose
melody he wasn't allowed to share. Beside the
motorway's eternal din, staring up at a fading
day, I knew we were weary. We thought we were
sound. Pretending to be wet.

Remembrance Day

1977

Whale Bay/ gasping/ from the shore/ I see him a
dark shadow underwater/ my feet are embedded
in the sand/ grains decorate my calves and ankles/
a zodiac map/ I continue/ counting/ onward/
through fifty/ or until he lifts his lips out of the
sea/ salt/ air/ a son losing his perfection.

2004

Summer.
London tube: a colon of cultural waste waiting to
exit the other side.

A woman pressed against the doors, black like a
new island potato pot, her eyes cast down. There's
nothing to stare into except the ads for cheap
flights to an isle she thought she had escaped.
Clutching onto a beauty even her mother would
recognize from the another-world, she possesses
a glow that would convince me there's hope for us
all, despite the sweat.

She wears flowers today, patterns of potential.
There's no sun to lift their colourful heads off her
bosom. I feel most comfortable here underground,
screeching to a halt. Until I'm pushed out.

1977

Whale Bay/ sun setting behind a horizontal hope/
Whale Bay/ a wonderland for plastic warriors and
worries/ my father breaks the blue/ he/ turtle/
confident that he knows home/ a love/ father to
sun/ I am learning of Turtlemen/ heads bobbing
up/ out/ breaching blue movements of music
that push the globe dizzy/ a love/ father to son/
it is these lost seconds that I wish mother's skirt
flip-flap out again/ where borders blow/ against
the silence of my undeveloped heart/   / I wish
mother's skirts wept along my thighs/ tangled
around my knees/ playing flag masses around my
square hips/ fastening my waist/ anchor/ a love

father/ I want him/ as the sand needs feet to give
it form/ as a mouth needs a tongue so that it may
taste/ let him lift my skirts woven from the thread
of wooden wheels/ I want him to rush unto me/ a
wave breaking on the barrier.

2004

I cut my mother's skirt and make underwear. I
wear them at popular London aquariums with
reflections of neon light on the surface tension,
where I wait for wild men to dive hoping to
crack my shell. I lost my home a long time ago.

Turtlemen know how to drown long enough so they can crawl out onto the night beach, both heartache and home weighing upon their future.

I'm stitched into my mother's skirt, torn up and tailored to hold my balls against my skin. Stunned under laser lights and songs made for fucking, I go fishing for fathers dripping the ocean down their red forearms. I know I'm sexy – despite the sweat.

For a clearer look I place my head below the surface. I won't come up gasping for love. I will beat my father at drowning. It's always been a game of time.

1977

Whale boy/ playing dead on the surface/ flotsam floating out into the world made of television lights/ drowning is a game based on time/ my father rises out of the water/ he has found the perfection in drowning/ I play at it/ he hovers just below the line/ drowning just below the skin/ then like granny's superstitions he rises/ a spell-ridden colossus/ an ocean trickling down his red forearms/ breeze kissing his shoulders/ a positive dance through the negative space I swallow/ 'you gotta learn to not kick at the water'/ become Turtlemen.

Week of the Dog

Here in London/ during that week/ I on the
southern end of the porcelain tub/ he on the
northern/ Our blue walls reflecting off the still
clear water/ we care not for summer shortage/
Steal we do guiltless moments/ Highbury
humming around us/ the water grows to
chill/ seven days our bodies lie baptized
silent underneath / He lathers and washes
my mess of hair/ I shudder under the jug.

Return of the Selkie

My last love was found tucked in the pocket of
an old Selkie from the bays of Scotland. Every
so often he would miss the waters of Dundee
and unwrap from under our bed a thrice-folded,
worn, sealskin cloak. He would throw it around his
slender shoulders, slide toward the tub and run
the Thames through a tap. He'd slap and chuckle
and clap his hands, lean to kiss me, tickle my lip
with his white wet whiskers. I could smell the
aged, sweet, dried salt on his pelt and I'd touch his
rolling ribs beneath it and pull him close.

One Monday morning with the larks' laughter my
beast grew thinner. As the sun perched herself on
the shelf for the rising, and as I typed poems out
of recycled paper yesterdays, after almost half a
century, a flickering light in his eyes heralded him
back. He transformed on our kitchen floor with a
thousand small tremors.

Saturday. Fixed with tubes and morphine. 3:36pm.
I turned my head away from him as a swimmer
does reaching for air. In the immensity between
those light-pulsed seconds my old Selkie dived
and fiercely trembled free. Within that dark
cerulean, the slowing of the hand through the
wave, I failed to carry him to the ocean-side, to let
him grow accustomed to the cold North Sea again.

I wasn't there to wail 'swim, swim' to support him from under his belly as he kicked out toward the estuary. I wasn't there to whisper our secrets into the ebb or whistle. Or whistle. Or whistle.

Lay Me on Us

lay me on us
let I shiver
wait at once

these wounds
these wounds

this weeping ours
will stop

these wounds
these wounds

these knotted
names will with
echoes go.

Note: traditional Turtlemen prayer

It's Beautiful What's Happening to Us.

SCENE: The sweet smell of new death is common in these quarters. Five beds wait in this room. The sixth takes comfort in being used. There is a window; outside hills roll in and to the west a sliver of blue sea.

THE OLD OLD MAN: It's almost time. Almost.

THE NURSE: [Enters] Time to get ready.

THE OLD OLD MAN: Can you pass me my wig?

THE NURSE: [Lifts the tightly curled wig off the Styrofoam head next to his bed]

THE OLD OLD MAN: My lips.

THE NURSE: [Gently twists a small cosmetic vial revealing an ancient red tip]

THE OLD OLD MAN: [Quivering hands like those of a wet child, he draws his lips and kisses the ghost]

THE NURSE: Your dress?

THE OLD OLD MAN: Not that old thing. Behind the door. My green suit. It's new.

[The Nurse retrieves an emerald velvet three-piece suit, a weary reminder of dazzle. She dresses him as a granddaughter would: first his crisp white shirt; then one sock at a time; his trousers, then belt; ties his bowtie, buttons his vest, and finally one slow arm at a time into his jacket]

THE NURSE: Your brogues?

THE OLD OLD MAN: No dear, my heels.

THE NURSE: [Collecting a small mirror from the corner near the visitor's chair. She stands in front of him] Stunning.

[Pause]

THE OLD OLD MAN: He's picking me up at noon. It's near.

THE NURSE: If I could be as lucky as you.

THE OLD OLD MAN: Look dear, can you see him, on the rooftop, standing. His brown wedding suit. So handsome. It's almost time to go.

[He waves 'come' toward the window. His eyes misty in anticipation]

THE NURSE: Let me help you into bed.

THE OLD OLD MAN: No No, I'll wait here. He will see me best standing nearest the station.

THE NURSE: [Exit]

THE OLD OLD MAN: [Shimmers and waits]

LEXICON

Baygrapes (*Coccoloba uvifera*) Believed to have reached Bermuda as seeds along the gulf stream from the Caribbean and Florida coast, these bittersweet yet hardy grapes grow quite plentifully along the southern shore. They are valued for their wood, which can be used to make charcoal, and for their ornamental leaves that are never far from a child's art project, Bermuda Day float or a wedding banquet table.

Bermuda Easter Lilies (*Lilium Longiflorum var. Eximium*) Introduced to the island around 1850s from Japan, Bermuda Lilies were being cultivated from the 1920s till shortly after WW2 for export. Though once described as growing like weeds around Bermuda, today they may not be as plentiful but there always seems to be enough to send the British monarch a bouquet every easter.

Bermuda Onions (*Sweet Onions*) Agriculture in Bermuda expanded greatly in the 1800s with the migration of Madeiran and Azorean skilled farmers. These labourers brought with them the seeds of a mild variety of onion. And those seeds mixed with Bermuda soil and climate created the highly sought-after, large, sweet onion which Bermuda then exported globally. Bermuda became known as the 'Onion Patch' and locals affectionately called themselves 'Onions', and some still do today. Unfortunately, after WW1 large-scale production dropped when the Americans figured out they could grow them in Texas.

Loquats (*Eriobotrya Japonica*) Introduced to Bermuda from Asia in 1850 to prevent birds eating local grapefruits and oranges. What wasn't anticipated were locals foraging for the fruit: kids climbing trees for the juiciest at the top, grown adults trespassing on not-so-neighbouring properties to gather enough for a few pots of jelly and families taking a Sunday stroll picking wild bunches along the old railway trails.

Surinam Cherry (*Eugenia uniflora*) No one is exactly sure when the Surinam Cherry was introduced to Bermuda. The scrub or small tree can grow to about 15 feet high with bright red cherries. As with loquats, Bermudians will go exploring for them during cherry season – returning home with stained hands and pockets, and plastic bags, sandwich boxes or anything filled or empty depending on how long the journey back home is.

Loons (also known as Divers) You can find these aquatic birds in North America and northern Eurasia. Revered by the Canadians, despite not being crowned the national bird – the gray jay holds that title – loons are bestowed with the honour of being cast onto the dollar coins, which are also called 'Loonies'. And just like Canadians, do not mistake loons for docile creatures: in 2019 an American bald eagle was found floating dead in a lake; after forensic examination it was declared stabbed through the heart by the beak of a loon.

Selkies (Seal folk) Mythological Scottish beings that can shed their seal skin to expose their human form. The tales often tell of a man who steals a selkie woman's skin to force her into becoming his wife and the woman spends her years in captivity longing and staring at the ocean.

Whales Whaling was first recorded in Bermuda around 1616 (seven years after the British first crashed into Bermuda); it was also recorded that we weren't very good at it. By 1660 it had become valuable due to the export of whale oil. Whaling boats would be made up of mixed crews of white sailors and skilled slaves; at its height a skilled slave Harpooner would be paid £2 per killing. Whaling seemed to end in the 1940s. Though right whales, sperm whales and orcas were once caught, it is mainly humpbacks that are still spotted migrating past Bermuda today.

Bermuda Riots 1977 In 1973 the Bermuda Governor and aide-de-camp were assassinated a few months after the murder of the Police Commissioner in 1972. In 1977 two men stood trial for their murders as well as the murder of two shop keepers (also in 1972). They were found guilty and sentenced to death by hanging on the morning of 2 December 1977. An explosive combination of race and lack of trust in the justice system, as well as other political and social issues, ignited. Demonstrations were followed by riots over several nights resulting in deaths and the deployment of the Bermuda Regiment, and US and UK troops.

Sarah (Sally/Sary) Bassett In the grounds of the Cabinet Office, Hamilton, Bermuda, in 2008, a ten-foot statue was erected of a woman who to this day remains a symbol of familial love, resistance to slavery and steadfastness in the face of death. In 1730 Sarah Bassett was found guilty of conspiring to poison the slaveholders of her granddaughter Beck. She was sentenced to be burnt at the stake at Crow Lane, a busy intersection into the city. She was reported to have declared to the crowd on the way there 'No use you hurrying folks, there'll be no fun 'til I get there.' Since then, extremely hot days are often referred to as 'a Sally Bassett day' and folklore has it that out of her ashes grew a small blue iris, the *Bermudiana*, which blooms throughout the island.

the Variety Girls Cricket Team
in St. Georges. The day they played the St. Georg
Girls C. Club. Sept 1943.

ACKNOWLEDGEMENTS

Gratitude: Cherry Smyth, Alan C. Smith, kitt price, San Alland, Joao Trindade, Guy Harries, Cristina Petrella, Norris, Shannon & Steven Simons, The Bermuda Arts Council

Memoriam: my grandmother, Elaine Simons

Note: Variations of the following works have appeared in other publications – HURRICANE: Emily, Unca, The Killing Floor, Parting the Atlantic, Remembrance Day, Week of the Dog, Return of the Selkie

Common Intellectual series

Current Editions

Future Editions

For future editions, please visit the Copy Press website

Copy Press is committed to bringing readers and writers together and invites you to join its Reader's Union – please visit www.copypress.co.uk